THINGS TO DO NOW THAT YOU'RE 40

things to do now

REBECCA HALL   Illustrations by Robyn Neild

hat you're 40

spruce

contents

1 challenge yourself... 6

2 enrich your body and mind... 34

3 go back to nature... 62

4 review your achievements... 98

5 celebrate your creativity... 128

6 upgrade your attitude... 152

7 refresh your soul... 178

8 re-evaluate your relationships... 216

challenge
yourself

Drive through a foreign city in an open-topped sports car, feeling the wind in your hair.

Explore the underwater world, either by scuba diving, snorkeling, or sailing in a glass-bottomed boat.

Do something scandalous that will shock your descendants one day.

Party all night long and through the next day without stopping to sleep.

Give your friends something to gossip about.

*Adopt an unusual, unexpected hobby
—the more bizarre, the better.*

*Ride on the back of a motorcycle
along country lanes at night.*

Ride to the top
of a skyscraper in
a glass elevator.

*Go traveling with a backpack
containing just one change of clothes.
Stay off the beaten track, eat local
food, and enjoy living simply.*

Drive your dream car. If you can't
afford to buy it, take a showroom
model for a test drive.

Ride a cable car to a mountaintop and take in the panoramic views.

Try waterskiing, windsurfing, jetskiing, or wakeboarding before your forty-first birthday.

Go to a fancy party dressed up as your favorite historical character.

Fly in a helicopter, a glider, or a hot-air balloon.

Try the scariest ride in a theme park (and take a sickness bag).

Plan to do a bungee jump or a parachute jump before you're fifty—if that's something you've wanted to do.

Celebrate Kwanzaa, Hanukkah, Chinese New Year, or any major festival from a culture that's not your own.

Have at least one spectacular New Year as part of a huge crowd; for example, go to Times Square in New York, Trafalgar Square in London, or Copacabana Beach in Rio.

Ride in a pedicab, a sleigh drawn by huskies, a horse-drawn carriage, or on a tandem bike.

Try abseiling, paragliding, or parasailing.

Go camping with friends and at night tell ghost stories around the campfire.

Walk across a rope bridge over a ravine.

Perfect a couple of party tricks you can use to entertain a crowd.

" We should consider every day lost on which we have not danced at least once. "
FRIEDRICH NIETZSCHE

Show a visitor around your hometown and view it as a tourist for a day.

Play roulette in a casino and lose more money than you can afford.

Splash out and enjoy a "how the other half lives" experience. Fly first class, drink champagne at the Ritz, or order lobster and caviar in a top seafood restaurant.

Dress up in costume and join a carnival parade.

Attempt to overcome your greatest fear. If it's heights, take a mountaineering course; if it's snakes, go to a zoo where they'll let you hold one.

Slide down a banister.

Play Twister with close friends
(cocktails will help loosen up everyone).
You'll be even closer when you finish!

Try to visit at least one of the Seven Wonders of the World.

" The time has come for me to
get my kite flying, stretch out in
the sun, kick off my shoes, and
speak my piece. "
HARPO MARX

*Borrow a skateboard and get a kid to
teach you some basic moves.*

Invent a gadget that would make
your life easier, then patent it.

Ride on an elephant or a camel.

Pretend to be someone you're
not for a day.

Spread a map on the table, shut
your eyes, and point. Then go to
the place you pointed at.

Try to find the pot of gold at
the end of a rainbow.

*"The voyage of discovery is not in seeking
new landscapes but in having new eyes."*
MARCEL PROUST

Organize a luxurious picnic for a very special friend.

Attend at least one huge rock concert or festival, where you are a tiny speck among tens of thousands of others.

Take a potluck vacation. Decide on your dates and your budget, then see what your travel agent comes up with.

Do any traveling that is going to involve slumming it before you're fifty. As you get older, a bed and a hot shower are harder to do without.

Eat a meal in a restaurant by yourself.

Have a drink in a bar alone,
and chat with the bartender.

Go to a restaurant that serves a cuisine you know little about and ask the waiter to choose your meal for you.

Make a complete and utter fool
of yourself and don't think twice
about who witnessed the spectacle
or what they might think.

Try to get your driver's license before you're
forty-five, if you don't have it already. It makes
new places much more accessible.

*Visit the birthplace of your
favorite kind of music, whether
it's Nashville, New Orleans,
Memphis, or Liverpool.*

Try to get a sense of what life is like in new places, instead of hanging out by the hotel pool.

> *" Do something for the joy of doing it and pray you won't be punished. "*
> SAMMY CAHN

Audition for a TV reality show!

Change your name if you don't like the one you were given.

Ride up a mountain in a chair lift.

Try skiing at some point.

Learn ballroom dancing and spend an evening waltzing to a big band.

Learn how to make a decent martini—shaken or stirred.

" Avoiding danger is no safer in the long run than outright exposure. Life is either a daring adventure, or nothing. "

HELEN KELLER

Put a message in a bottle and throw it out to sea.

Keep looking for that four-leaf clover.

Make love on a forest floor, breathing in the essence of the trees.

Launch your second childhood now, while you've still got the muscle tone and mobility to truly push the envelope.

Don't just dream about it: get out there and give it a go.

"When choosing between two evils, I always like to try the one I've never tried before."

MAE WEST

*If you ever get the chance,
do something truly heroic.*

Upgrade your vices: drink better wines, splurge on better seats at concerts, and eat "luxury" foods from time to time.

Spend a night in a haunted house and be open to the idea that ghosts really do exist.

Read up on UFOs
and then see if you
can spot one.

Spend a day sightseeing with a child and try to find the same innocence that once existed within you.

Join the mile-high club or at least kiss someone passionately at thirty-thousand feet.

Watch airplanes flying overhead and try to guess where they're going.

Compose your own ringtone for your cell phone.

Learn the lyrics and dance moves to a current pop song.

Perform in a karaoke bar.

" The aging process has you firmly in its grasp if you never get the urge to throw a snowball. "
DOUG LARSON

Buy an antique and
trace its history.

Walk without a destination in mind.
Flip a coin at the end of every street
to determine your direction.

Teach an old dog a new trick.

Go somewhere you always thought you didn't want to go, and open your mind to it.

Listen to weird radio stations
in the middle of the night.

Eat too much cotton candy and popcorn
at an amusement park or county fair.

*"You're only given a little spark
of madness. You mustn't lose it."*
ROBIN WILLIAMS

Do a cartwheel across the
dance floor in a nightclub.

Learn how to fly a kite.

Go bowling and give it your all.

 Try all the slot machines in an amusement arcade.

Visit a magic store and buy tricks for any friends who'll appreciate them.

Take a rowboat down a river on a lazy afternoon.

Gallop a horse along a beach at dusk.

Run a marathon, or a half marathon, or a quarter marathon—or just the length of your road—the key is to challenge your limits.

Strike up a conversation with the passenger next to you on a longhaul flight.

Go with a friend to a cheesy nightclub in another town and dance your socks off.

Send a drink to a stranger at the other end of a bar.

Consider this: even if life is not the party we hoped for, while we're here we should dance.

*Make sure you have danced
with an attractive stranger
whose name you don't know.*

"The follies which a man regrets most
in his life are those which he didn't
commit when he had the opportunity."
HELEN ROWLAND

Take a vacation on
your own at least once.

*Make a list of the five places in the world you
most want to see and plan how you are going
to get there.*

Revisit your childhood activities.
Have you forgotten how to skip,
use a hula hoop, or scale a jungle
gym? It's not too late!

*Ask for the moon as well—
even when you've got the stars.*

*Be an extra in a film and
maneuver yourself into the
foreground of the shot.*

Go on a protest march. Stand up
for something you believe in.

Sign petitions, lobby your
congresspeople, get involved.

Have a mid-life adventure instead of a crisis.

Try swinging upside
down on a trapeze.

*Get a backstage pass and meet
the band after a rock concert.*

*Go on different kinds of
boats, including a paddle
steamer, a canoe, and
a fishing boat.*

Start an eclectic collection.

Go to a baseball, basketball, or soccer game—even if you're not interested in sports. Feel the energy and excitement, and listen to the roar of the crowd.

> All animals except man know that the ultimate point of life is to enjoy it.
> SAMUEL BUTLER

Make sure you've had your fair share of vacations—or more than your fair share.

Cause trouble. According to George Bernard Shaw, that's what life is all about. Make sure you've caused enough.

*Stir things up if they
are going too smoothly.*

Find ways to make
yourself feel younger.

" Let your hook always be
cast; in the pool where
you least expect it,
there will be a fish. "
OVID

*Decide which actor you want to
play you in the movie of your life.*

*Dance the cancan, the hula,
or do Cossack kicks.*

Reject the mediocre and
aim for the extraordinary.

*Look for comets or visible planets in
the night sky, when they are going to
be observable, and don't go to bed
until you have spotted them.*

*Throw caution to the wind.
Take risks.*

Don't be afraid to break the rules sometimes,
so long as it doesn't harm anyone else.

Never miss a party. If it's boring you can leave early, but if you don't go you won't know.

Choose a date when you throw a party every year. Make it your trademark.

Take heed of these words from *Peter Pan*:
You can fly so long as you have happy thoughts.

Drop the act. Be yourself and be proud of it.

enrich your body and mind

Learn to love your body and feel comfortable in your skin.

Get personal grooming down to a fine art so you can look your best in the least possible time.

Make sure someone irresistible has licked your stomach and kissed the backs of your knees.

Improve your posture, and watch the years fall away. (It will also make your stomach look flatter.)

Don't accept fatigue—get your body back on course with a good dose of multivitamins.

Try some complementary therapies, even if it's just arnica for bruises or valerian for insomnia.

Learn the Chinese art of tongue diagnosis and see what yours tells you about your overall health.

Have an oxygen facial for pure, refreshed, ultra-clean skin.

Buy a juicer and make your own fresh juices (but try to get someone else to clean it).

Adopt at least one crazy hairstyle or hair color, or both.

Buy a luxuriously comfortable sofa or armchair for total relaxation.

Try some Périgord truffles, Jerusalem artichokes, and durian fruit.

Bathe in champagne or perfumed water strewn with rose petals.

Spend more than you can afford on an outfit that will take you anywhere.

Try hypnotherapy; it is an eye-opening experience that can help to shift negative behavior patterns.

If you smoke, make sure you've given up by your next birthday.

Smile every morning before you get out of bed.

Find the form of dance that suits your natural rhythm and your taste in music, be it tango, jive, salsa, or belly dancing.

Pick up just enough medical knowledge so you're able to listen to your body and understand when it's telling you to take care.

Devise your own strategies for fighting off colds.

Get a saucy tattoo! If you don't want to go this far, use a wash-off transfer and have a photo taken to show your grandchildren.

Have your color chart done and buy something in the shade that suits you best.

" Middle age is when your age starts to show around your middle. "

BOB HOPE

Don't relax into middle age; at forty you can still be a big kid if you choose.

Start taking care of yourself, and plan to live a long, healthy life.

Eat some vegetables every day, even if you don't like them.

Make a plaster cast of the part of your body you like best. Display it as an objet d'art in your home.

Get a pedicure and take pride in your toes.

Treat yourself to cosmetic dentistry, so you've got a set of even, sparkly white teeth. It's one of the best ways to look younger.

Caryn Leschen once said, "Thirty-five is when you finally get your head together and your body starts falling apart." Prove her wrong.

*Learn a morning stretch routine, before
you get too creaky to put your socks on.*

*Find a sport you enjoy
and get proficient at it.*

Take a first-aid course, so you
know what to do in an emergency.

Put some time and energy
into solving any niggling
health problems you have
before your next birthday.

*Take a sunny afternoon off work,
and sit outside and daydream.*

Do pelvic floor exercises daily, whether you're a man or a woman, to avoid bladder-control problems in the future.

Keep a photo handy showing you in a swimsuit when you were at your ideal weight. Resolve to keep that figure (or regain it).

Discover the therapeutic benefits of massage; it's great for stress relief.

Learn how to give a good massage, and you'll always be popular.

Harness your sex appeal and use it wisely.

Resolve to laugh as much as possible and if, at the end of a day, you realize you haven't laughed at all, get someone to tickle you.

Frequent at least one local bar or restaurant where the staff know you by name.

Practice eye-muscle exercises to prolong your eyesight (ask your optician if you don't know how).

Learn to do sit-ups without straining your spine. Don't let that potbelly establish itself.

Have you changed your dress style since your twenties? If not, it could be time.

Introduce a couple of new colors into your wardrobe, especially if you always wear the same ones.

Go through your wardrobe and get rid of anything you haven't worn in the last year. This is no time for sentimentality!

Delete those micro-miniskirts from your wardrobe; however, if an objective friend swears you still look good in yours, by all means keep them.

Stop going to parties filled with twentysomethings; it's not good for the ego.

Adopt a defining characteristic people can describe you by.

 *Try a detox diet to cleanse away years of hard living.*

Find a pair of sunglasses that makes you look really cool.

Figure out the foods that make your digestive system work most efficiently.

Start using moisturizer and sunscreen regularly to keep your skin supple.

When asked on his deathbed about his greatest regret, John Betjeman said, "I didn't have enough sex." Don't let this happen to you.

*Do a walk or run for charity
in a ridiculous costume.*

Make friends with your spinal
column! Learn to roll down
very slowly and touch your
toes, then straighten up
again, vertebra by vertebra.

Get sleep. Make your bed a
haven of peace and comfort,
and find your own infallible
ways of falling asleep.

Find out what foods you're allergic to and avoid them.

If you're not already at your target weight, set yourself a goal and make a big effort to get there. Losing weight becomes harder the older you get.

Have a day of exotic pampering, with seaweed wraps and algae Jacuzzis. You'll definitely be back for more once you've tried it.

Cook a curry from scratch, grinding the spices with a mortar and pestle.

Make a conscious decision not to become a middle-aged slob. Even when you're not going anywhere, dress nicely and groom yourself. You never know who's going to be around the corner...

Make your motto for your fortieth year: live for today, plan for tomorrow, party tonight.

> **Better keep yourself clean and bright; you are the window through which you must see the world.**
>
> GEORGE BERNARD SHAW

If you tend to hunch over your desk or slump in front of the TV, it's time to change your habits before they cause long-term damage. Learn Pilates or the Alexander technique.

Have a professional photographer take some portraits of you looking sensational.

Get an artist to paint you looking sensational—even better!

Try to live without wearing a watch. You may discover that your body has an inner clock you can rely on.

Know that when it comes to decoration, less is more.

Give up sunbathing to avoid the leather handbag look.

Get into the habit of buying yourself a present every week. You deserve it!

Have a float in a flotation tank.

Buy an exercise ball and learn how to use it.

Eat your breakfast outdoors in summer.

Borrow a pedometer to find out how far you walk in an average day.

Freeze your eggs in case you decide to have a baby in your late forties.

Get up early enough to have a calm start to the day, and include something nurturing in your morning routine.

*Learn to breathe fully and freely,
giving your body plenty of oxygen.*

James Thurber said, "Women
deserve to have more than
twelve years between the ages
of twenty-eight and forty."
Make sure you try.

*Make it a rule to drink eight glasses of
water a day to refresh and detoxify.*

*Buy an ionizer for all the rooms you
spend a lot of time in, so the air is
energizing rather than draining.*

Resolve that you will touch your toes
every day for the rest of your life.

Do enough exercise before you're forty; your enhanced muscle definition will stand you in good stead later.

Find a hat that suits you.

Develop your own distinctive style, and then alter it from time to time.

Don't start choosing clothes purely for comfort yet— you're far too young for that.

Find a couple of favorite clothes shops; this will make shopping trips more efficient.

Sleep naked or in something sexy;
shapeless pajamas and tent-style
nighties are for the over-sixty set.

Appreciate beauty in others, whether they're
friends, lovers, or strangers on a train.

*Experiment with
aromatherapy and notice
the way the different oils
can change your mood.*

*Listen to your biorhythms. Work out when
your energy levels are highest, and use this
information to be more productive.*

Insist on the best when it matters.

Find a hairstylist who is at least ten years younger than you and give them carte blanche.

Donate blood regularly.

Sign the form to donate your organs when you die.

Find a cure for something that ails you, and broadcast your tips on the Internet.

Visit an osteopath or a chiropractor and get your bones cracked.

Decide on your favorite smells, and seek them out.

Tape yourself sleeping to find out if you snore.

Start monitoring your facial expressions so you acquire laughter rather than frown lines.

Teach yourself to sleep on your back, so your face isn't squashed and so wrinkles don't form while you're sleeping.

Fast for a day just to see what it feels like.

Bite into a hot chili pepper – just once.

Buy organic food; eliminate unhealthy preservatives and other chemicals from your diet.

Eat sea vegetables, such as wakame, hijiki, kombu, and nori; they're rich in vitamins and minerals, and they taste good too.

Decide on your best physical assets and dress to emphasize them.

Collect compliments. Note what other people appreciate about you.

Determine which of the following is most important: beauty, success, health, wealth, or happiness. Have your priorities changed since your twenties?

Get good at making eye contact; it will allow you to communicate more effectively.

" I'm not 40; I'm 18 with 22 years' experience. "
ANONYMOUS

Get yourself a warm coat to keep out the cold.

If you plan to start lying about your age, why not do it in style and throw a second fortieth birthday party.

Be very grateful that wrinkles don't hurt.

Accept that there is no point in fighting gravity.

Get a full-length mirror, so you can see yourself below the waist.

Collect some good-quality classic outfits for each season.

Revise your style of beachwear, and arrange mirrors so you can check the back view before you venture out.

Remember: you're only physically young once, but you can stay mentally young indefinitely.

Eat well, but don't get too serious about it. You can still choose your cereal based on the plastic toy inside rather than the fiber content.

" Age is an issue of mind over matter. If you don't mind, it doesn't matter. "
MARK TWAIN

Found some gray hairs? Decide if you suit them and, if you don't, fix them.

Don't let anyone else find out how vain you are.

Realize that good looks aren't the be-all and end-all, but learn to make the most of what you've been given.

Be aware that your prime starts now.

go back
to nature

Watch a sunrise from the top of a mountain.

Learn how to whistle through a blade of grass.

Strike up a relationship with an animal and make sure you understand each other, however briefly.

Sail out on the ocean until you can't see any land, or other boats.

Watch a sunset from a cliff looking out over an ocean.

Learn how to skim stones across a pond.

Feed a baby animal from a bottle.

Plant a tree in your backyard or in the countryside, and watch it grow.

Plant some wildflower seeds in a field.

Learn to distinguish the North Star, the Big Dipper, and Orion in the night sky.

Go skinny-dipping in the moonlight with someone special.

Lie on your back in a forest, look up through the branches, and listen to the trees.

Blow the spores of a dandelion and make a wish.

Know how to light
a fire with dry
sticks, in case you
ever get stranded
on a desert island.

Learn how to tell the time using a sundial.

Make it your goal to
know the names of forty
different plants or trees.

Hug a tree during daylight hours and feel it transmit the strength of the earth. Tree-hugging at night is said to sap your energy, so better to do it during the day.

Sow your wild oats.

Learn to distinguish twelve different herbs by scent alone.

Roast marshmallows over a campfire as the sun is setting.

Go fishing and eat
whatever you catch.

*Stand outside in a torrential rainstorm
until you're soaked to the skin.*

Go for a country walk just after
the rain has stopped and notice all
the different scents in the air.

*Everyone should swim with
dolphins at some stage in their
life——the sooner the better.*

Feed the birds or any other small animals that come to your garden or local park.

Stand under a waterfall and let nature cleanse you.

Find a stone at the beach with a hole that goes right through it. Take it home with you to ward off witches.

Try to see a lunar or solar eclipse. Imagine how scary it would have been before planetary movements were understood.

Grow herbs on your kitchen windowsill, and learn about their therapeutic as well as culinary uses.

Become aware of the phases of the moon. Note how they change the way you feel.

Learn a bird call and use it in the wild.

Lie on your back and watch the clouds with someone. Find pictures in them; see if your friend can see the same ones.

Learn to milk a cow. You never know
when you might need this skill.

Think of your favorite animal.
Have you seen one close up yet?

Mix your own
cement and build
a stone wall.

Go vegetarian for a month.
You might decide to stick to it.

Climb a tree and sit in its branches.

Spend plenty of time outdoors to keep you aware of the changing seasons.

Try to notice the exact day when summer turns to autumn or winter turns to spring.

Make a collection of natural objects: seashells, pressed flowers or leaves, or beautiful stones.

Make a loaf of bread from scratch.

Walk barefoot through soft, warm mud.

Learn how to row a boat.

Know how to recognize the song of a blackbird, a nightingale, and a sparrow.

Sunbathe naked in a secluded spot.

*Go whale watching and
take lots of photographs.*

Find the landscape
that speaks to your
soul, whether it be
mountain or ocean,
desert or forest.

Find a fairy ring
and make a wish.

Pick some wild mushrooms, check they're not poisonous, then cook and eat them.

Go to a flower market first thing in the morning and buy one perfect bloom.

Go to a spice market in a hot country and inhale the aromas.

Sing your favorite song at the top of your lungs on a deserted beach.

*Sit quietly in the middle of a
desert and listen to the wind.*

Know that you're never too old
for a water fight, a toboggan ride,
or a bounce on a trampoline.

Examine the patterns
on a butterfly's wings.

*Look at a spider's web
first thing in the morning
when it is dotted with dew.*

Spend half an hour watching a colony of ants at work.

Read a book in a tree.
Don't tell anyone where you are.

Go to a farm and pick your own fruit.

Make homemade lemonade on a hot day.

Change a baby's diaper.

Eat the smelliest cheese you can find.

Use a piece of string
to tease a kitten.

*Turn your face to the sky
and let rain fall on it.*

Try to see the aurora borealis.

Wish on a falling star.

Wash your clothes in a stream and dry them on a rock.

 Go fossil hunting in an area of geological interest.

Have a star named after you.

Adopt a donkey in a sanctuary or an animal in a zoo, and send it a card on its birthday.

Make a daisy chain.

Have a mud bath and roll around in it.

Go to a winery and tread grapes to make your own wine.

Rescue an insect from drowning.

Swim in a river, a lake, a sea, and an ocean.

Grow your own tomatoes, zucchinis, or carrots.

Watch animals in the wild, when they don't know they're being watched.

Learn how to seize a rose without getting pricked by its thorns.

Walk barefoot along beaches; notice how different types of sand feel between your toes.

Develop your internal compass so you get good at knowing which way is north.

> Once we no longer live beneath our mother's heart, it is the earth with which we form the same dependent relationship, relying...on its cycles and elements, helpless without its protective embrace.
> LOUISE ERDRICH

Float on your back in the ocean and watch the changing sky above.

Catch a snowflake on your tongue and let it melt.

Walk through an ancient forest and feel the primeval atmosphere.

*Visit a botanic garden and admire
exotic plants from other countries.*

Make it your goal to live more
in tune with the environment.

Take a moment to count
all the different shades
of green outside.

*Eat a perfectly ripe piece of fruit and
let the juice run down your chin.*

Feed a bird breadcrumbs
from the palm of your hand.

*Sit on the cool grass
and wriggle your toes.*

Try to get a parrot to say your name.

*Spend at least part of the day
outside on your birthday.*

*Resolve to eat local fruits and vegetables in
season, rather than ones that are flown in
from the other side of the world, thus
polluting the atmosphere with jet fuel.*

Take a dog for a long walk in the countryside and run alongside it.

Make a wish on a rainbow; if you see a double rainbow, celebrate, because you will be lucky all that day.

Plant some bulbs that will flower the following year. They'll remind you how quickly time passes, because the shoots will appear in no time.

Watch how hard bees work when they are collecting nectar from flowers.

Bury your nose in an open rose and breathe in its scent—unless you are allergic!

Chew a blade of grass; you might be surprised how tasty grass is.

Take a walk on a windy day and feel the gusts blowing away all your cobwebs.

Get really good at relaxing.
Make it one of your specialties.

Stroke a baby's cheek, smell its hair, and kiss its nose.

Jump into puddles and enjoy the splash.

Rub your hand against an old stone wall and feel the texture. Some people believe stone holds memories over the centuries.

Wash your hair in pure
rainwater and feel the silkiness.

See if you can watch an egg hatching.

*Squash a ripe berry on
the roof of your mouth
and feel the juices explode.*

Listen to pigeons cooing at twilight.

Spend some time looking at the patterns ice makes on a windowpane.

Try to capture a flavor of each season as it passes.

Rub a feather across your cheek.

Look for a place where you can see glow worms sparkle or fireflies dance.

Find a pure mountain stream, then lie on your stomach and take a drink.

Go exploring in underground caves and feel close to the center of the earth.

Listen to the echoes in a valley; shout your name and hear it resound back.

Get as near as you dare to a live volcano—or visit an extinct one.

Watch a storm at sea from the nearest safe place that allows you to see the flashes of lightning and the power of the waves.

Look at the different layers and colors in a piece of rock.

Hold a seashell to your ear and listen to the sea.

Dig for cockles or clams on a wet beach with your pants rolled up and the sand in your toes.

See if you can spot a bat swooping through the air at dusk.

Wrap up warmly and then watch a winter tide come in.

Run through a pile of dry leaves and feel them crunch beneath you.

Hold a snake, a lizard, or a frog.

Stroke a fluffy baby chicken.

Try making your own jam; you'll have a
taste of summer to sweeten the winter.

*Whittle something
from a piece of wood.*

Resolve to use fewer chemicals
in and around your home.

Make a meal from a foreign cuisine; for example, try rolling your own sushi.

Eat an apple that's just fallen from a tree, or raspberries from a bush.

Feed a sugar cube to a friendly pony.

Take a bicycle ride through
the countryside and watch the
world go by at a slower pace.

*Trade down to a smaller car if you own
one. Do your part to halt global warming.*

*Learn to respect Nature,
and understand that she
is far wiser than mankind
will ever fathom.*

review your achievements

Think about what you used to want to do when you were growing up. Have you done it yet?

Be able to earn your own living now that you're forty.

Develop a nose for sniffing out insincerity.

Learn how to interpret your dreams.

Have one major achievement
you are extremely proud of,
as well as loads of lesser ones.

*" I believe one of the most important
priorities is to do whatever we do as well
as we can. We should take pride in that. "*
VICTOR KIAM

Volunteer with a worthy organization.

Practice your flirting skills diligently;
pretend you are competing for an
Olympic gold medal.

Hone your advanced bedroom techniques. (If you don't feel you have them, start learning some!)

Become an expert at some kind of manual skill, such as carpentry, knitting, or pottery. In this technological age, it's very satisfying to go back to basics.

Be open to change and new opportunities. If you are invited to elope to Tahiti tomorrow, don't dismiss it out of hand.

Learn how to use a computer, if only to pick up e-mails.

Learn how to survive with little money. Everyone should live through a period when they're very short of cash.

Learn how to make a decent omelet, even if you don't enjoy cooking.

Sign up for a night class to learn about a subject you're embarrassed not to know more about.

" The secret of life is honesty and fair dealing. If you can fake that, you've got it made. "
GROUCHO MARX

Sort out your finances, pay off your student debts, and have a retirement plan well under way.

Update your résumé with new skills you've acquired. Add new skills every few years.

Try to find a job you enjoy.

Make sure you have at least as many ambitions at forty as you had at twenty-one.

Gain public-speaking experience—
it's a useful skill to have.

" **Promise yourself to live your**
life as a revolution and not
just a process of evolution. "
ANTHONY J. D'ANGELO

Practice swimming underwater for
the breadth of a swimming pool.

Be able to play at least one musical
instrument well enough to entertain—
even if it's just for children's parties.

Learn to play "Stairway to Heaven" on a guitar, or a Beethoven sonata on a piano.

Practice juggling three balls in the air and become proficient at it.

Learn to cook a special dish from a recipe passed on by a grandparent or old friend; teach it to a child.

Take a weekend motivational course; it might help you find extra personal strengths you can tap.

> **You're not a failure if you don't make it; you are a success if you try.**
> SUSAN JEFFERS

Learn to touch type with more than two fingers, if you can't already (take a speed course to learn). It will help when using a computer or typing your first novel.

Learn a foreign language, visit a country where it's spoken, and only speak in the new language for the entire time you're there.

Master a subject at which you wish you had excelled at school.

Realize that it is never too late to live the life you once imagined for yourself.

Get something you've written in print. If all else fails, write a letter to your local newspaper.

Decide whether you're in the right career or if you want to make a change. If a change is desired, make it.

Understand the basic tenets of all the major world religions.

Write down three goals you would like to achieve by the time you are forty-five and display the list in a prominent location.

Hone a fairground skill so you can win fluffy toys for any children present.

66 I have not failed. I've just found 10,000 ways that won't work. 99
THOMAS EDISON

Take up karate, t'ai chi, or another martial art, and learn to defend yourself.

Write your own "things to do before I die" list, and begin to check off each entry.

Look through the Guinness Book of World Records and find a record you can match or beat.

Try to finish any projects you've started then set aside. Either that or throw them away.

" *We must always change, renew, rejuvenate ourselves; otherwise, we harden.* "

GOETHE

Feel the fear and do it anyway: challenge yourself
to do something that makes you nervous.

> *I am always doing
> that which I can not
> do, in order that I may
> learn how to do it.*
> PABLO PICASSO

Learn how to preset your VCR to
record programs while you're out.

*Know that freedom is not
something you can be given;
it's something you have to take.*

Think about how you would feel if someone told you, "This is it. You are living up to your full potential and this is the most you will ever attain." If this upsets you, make changes to prove them wrong.

Get involved in your community, especially if there is something that bothers you. Write to the council and agitate for change. If all else fails, consider running for office yourself.

Create a financial nest egg that would be enough to see you through if you lost your job or were too sick to work for three months.

Know how to get stains out of carpets and clothing.

Be able to sew on a button
and take up a hem.

*Don't bother just to be better than
your contemporaries or predecessors.
Try to be better than yourself.*
WILLIAM FAULKNER

Admit what you're not good at—
and find ways to compensate.

Acquire a hobby that gives you pleasure.

Be aware of your special abilities and devote plenty of time to them.

Buy your home, if you can. Give yourself a stable base from which you can go out and be the person you want to be.

" To fly, we have to have resistance. "
MAYA LIN

Master a video game and challenge a child to play against you.

Learn how to manage your emotions; if you do you will become more intuitive and able to appreciate life's natural highs.

Apply to law or medical school if you've always wanted to be a lawyer or doctor. It's not too late!

Join the text-messaging generation and learn the shorthand.

Put your money where your mouth is.

Win a prize—any kind of prize.

> If you think you can, you can. And if you think you can't, you're right.
>
> HENRY FORD

Make sure you've stood up to at least one impossible boss. Stay composed (so you feel good about your ability to deal with difficult situations) and handle yourself with diplomacy (so you don't get fired).

Stand up for your rights, whether it's returning defective goods or defending your place in a line.

Brainstorm new business ideas with three or four entrepreneurial friends. Consider collaborating to start one of them.

Institute a sensible filing system for your financial documents so you can find that mortgage statement quickly.

" You don't get to choose how you're going to die. Or when. You can only decide how you're going to live. Now. "
JOAN BAEZ

Create a home that is relaxing, comfortable, and safe.

Start an investment portfolio and dabble in the stock market.

Learn to blow bubbles with bubblegum.

Construct a piece of furniture from a do-it-yourself kit.

Flex your brain muscles and feel your power.

Help a child with their homework, and make sure you can still remember the basics of trigonometry.

Become an expert in something unusual.

Reread your résumé. Sit back and feel proud at your achievements.

" The young do not know enough to be prudent, and therefore they attempt the impossible, and achieve it, generation after generation. "
PEARL S. BUCK

Start planning how you are going to achieve your dream future. Will your finances stretch? If not, visit a financial advisor and figure out how you can attain the money to live your dreams.

Don't be afraid of a mid-life career change; nowadays, few people stay at one job for their entire career.

Figure out how to negotiate multiple-choice pre-recorded telephone messages to get a human being on the end of the line.

Work out your political beliefs and consider whether you have any skills you can contribute to the party you support.

Spend your money wisely.
Remember the saying,
"Thrifty till fifty, plenty at seventy."

Know at least one card trick.

*Stop striving for things you
know you cannot possibly attain.*

*Master a few neuro-linguistic programming skills,
to improve your communication with others.*

Nurture your intellectual curiosity.
When you don't know something, look it up.

 Campaign for
legislation you
believe in.

Book a spontaneous, last-minute airline
ticket or vacation on the Internet.

Learn how to navigate the
Internet without picking up
viruses or ending up at
undesirable Web sites.

*Knuckle down if you don't feel
you make enough money yet.*

*Be able to rub your stomach and
pat your head simultaneously.*

*Get housework down to a
fine art, so you spend as
little time on it as possible.*

Don't be too hard on yourself. If you
don't succeed at something, perhaps
you've chosen the wrong goal.

Learn to read body language;
it's often more expressive than words.

66 How many cares one loses
when one decides not to be
something but to be someone. 99
COCO CHANEL

Determine to be debt-free, even if it
means downsizing and starting again.

Check that you can still do a
somersault—but mind your neck!

Make sure you can still ride a bike in your forties. Consider buying one to ride to work.

Develop your repertoire of funny faces and ways of making young children giggle.

Find what you need to perform at your peak level: a good night's sleep, clothing that makes you feel confident, or even a lucky rabbit's foot.

Make one major life change in your fortieth year.

*Perfect some strategies you
can use to get your own way.*

*Don't be afraid to say "I don't
know" sometimes. People who have an
opinion about everything are irritating.*

Read some of the great
philosophers and consider
which of their theories of
existence you agree with.

Develop a technique for getting rid of
door-to-door salespeople and telemarketers.

Have some excuses at your fingertips
for when you need to get off the hook.

*Subscribe to a different
newspaper or magazine for a
month, to get a fresh perspective.*

*Fix everything in your house
that is broken before your next
birthday. Alternatively, just
throw these things away.*

celebrate your creativity

Make at least one beautiful masterpiece
that is entirely your own work.

*Choose paint colors for your home,
or part of it, that aren't white or cream.*

Explore all your talents until you find the
one that gives you the most satisfaction.

Start writing your thoughts, observations, and feelings in a diary.

Frame a picture you've painted.

> Develop your eccentricities while you're young, so that as you get older people don't think you're going gaga.
>
> GEORGE BURNS

Write to your favorite celebrity saying why you admire him or her, and ask if you can meet. The person might even say yes.

Have your handwriting analyzed and see if you agree with the results.

Think about the saddest scene you can remember in a book or a movie. Work out why it moves you.

Get a pen and a piece of paper and start writing. Don't plan, but just see what comes out.

Donate worthy books you know you'll never read to charity.

Invent an original recipe and make it for some adventurous friends.

" *Be careful what you pretend to be because you are what you pretend to be.* "
KURT VONNEGUT

Read a book on feng shui, or book a session with a consultant, then reorganize your home to stop clutter from obstructing your vital energies.

Develop your psychic abilities. Try guessing who's on the phone before you pick it up.

Research the myths and legends
associated with your hometown.

Start a play-reading group
to channel your inner actor.

 Play in the snow: make snow
angels, throw snowballs, make
a snowman, and go sledding.

*Get someone to videotape you doing something
idiotic and send it off to a caught-on-camera TV
show, if you've never appeared on television.*

Call during a radio phone-in
segment and share your opinion.

Consider this: works of art we create in
our twenties tend to be about style and
superficial subjects, but by our late
thirties we should have lived enough to
introduce real depth and understanding.

*The be-all and end-all of life should not
be to get rich, but to enrich the world.*
B. C. FORBES

Try to recall your favorite book when
you were a child, at about the age of
eight. Go back and reread it, and
figure out what appealed to you.

*Visit the neighborhood you lived in as a
child and look for the secret places where
you used to play hide-and-seek.*

*Build a huge sandcastle,
complete with moat and turrets.*

Read the opening lines of *The Canterbury Tales*
to a child, or get their blood flowing with a
dramatic rendition of "If" by Rudyard Kipling.

*Read novels that describe life in other
cultures. If the places intrigue you,
make plans to visit the countries.*

*Try to see the originals of your favorite
paintings, wherever they are hung.*

Turn off your TV and keep
it off for at least a week.
Consider leaving it off for good.

Collect a pile of magazines and cut out all the articles that interest you; sort them into categories. You may find an idea for your next creative work this way.

Go to the opera, and sit through it without reading the explanatory notes.

Watch a ballet performance by a world-renowned company.

Listen to John Cage's "Four Minutes, 33 Seconds" performed live.

Build your own Web site; fill it with things that matter to you, and update it regularly.

Create your own time capsule with facts and features of your life and times. Bury it in a safe place in the wilderness.

Follow your feelings and they will lead you to your soul.

Sort through all your photographs, then put them in albums and label them.

Start keeping a journal. Be sure to include lots of gossipy anecdotes and racy details that will provide lively reading when you're eighty.

Learn how to cook a dozen dishes well—and make sure they come from a variety of different cultures.

Write a song——a ditty, a love song, anything that you can put to music and call your own.

Start your own band if you've always wanted to be in one. It's never too late! Check out the Internet or your local music shop for possible participants.

" You only live once—but if you work it right, once is enough. "
JOE E. LEWIS

Think about a topic for a novel. Everyone has one in them. What's yours?

Find a favorite poet who can express things in a way that touches you.

Go to a place where you had a blissful childhood vacation and let the memories overwhelm you.

Own at least one object simply because it is beautiful.

Buy something at an auction, using sign language to make your bids.

Determine what it would take to make your home the place of your dreams.

Read an example of every genre of novel: romance, detective, sci-fi, adventure, thriller, and so on.

Keep a notebook in which you jot down your creative ideas.

Customize a T-shirt with your own design, logo, or slogan.

Add a unique design feature in your home: a beautiful piece of driftwood attached to one wall, a table decorated with sea glass, or any other imaginative idea you come up with.

Make a list of your ten favorite books, films, pieces of music, and paintings.

Think about this: Shakespeare wrote **Hamlet** *before his fortieth birthday; Beethoven had composed his "9th Symphony;" and Picasso had painted "Les Desmoiselles d'Avignon." What's your greatest work so far?*

Learn how to spend a whole day reading a novel without feeling guilty.

Visit your nearest art school end-of-year show and buy a work from one of the students. It could be a great investment.

Perfect the art of daydreaming.

> If I had to live my life again, I would make a rule to read some poetry and listen to some music at least once a week; for perhaps the parts of my brain now atrophied would thus have been kept active through use.
>
> CHARLES DARWIN

Listen to plays on the radio, rather than opting for a music, news, or sports channel every time.

Design an outfit for yourself and have it made by a tailor or dressmaker.

Diversify your music collection. Be sure it includes works in a range of categories and reflects your taste.

> " If you want to make your
> dreams come true, wake up.
> Wake up to your own strength.
> Wake up to the role you play
> in your own destiny. "
> KEITH ELLIS

Make a stained glass window and hang it where the sun will catch it every day.

Describe to a child under five what you do for a living.

Try glass-blowing, if you have the opportunity.

Collect an imaginative bundle of items—feathers, glitter, cotton, seaweed, dried flowers, and so on. Give the materials to a child with some paper and glue and ask her or him to make a collage.

Try to remember a favorite outfit from your childhood, then your favorite toy, favorite food, and favorite people.

Give a themed dinner party; include foods, table settings, music, and conversation that reflect the theme.

Do something creative while sitting outside during a full moon. It's a powerful experience.

Give your imagination free rein when decorating at least one room of your house.

Read all the Pulitzer Prize-winning novels of the last ten years.

Do something described by a favorite writer; for example, go to Walden Pond and drift in a canoe, or wander through a field of daffodils, like Wordsworth.

Find at least one friend or family member with whom you can correspond by letter writing—the old-fashioned way. Buy a special fountain pen to write your letters.

Try alternative forms of self-expression. If you enjoy painting, try sculpting; if you like writing poetry, try writing music.

Find your muse—the people, places, or activities that inspire you.

Have your portrait drawn by a cartoonist to see which features they decide to exaggerate.

Make an artwork out of found objects.

Be able to recite at least one poem by heart.

Memorize a dozen favorite quotations and work them into everyday conversations.

Give imaginative presents to your loved ones. Don't be predictable.

Stretch your brain cells: read difficult books and watch documentaries about complex subjects.

Buy yourself a decent camera and learn how to take good pictures.

Throw a party where you play only the music you danced to as a teenager and invite everyone to dance; see if guests revert to teenage behaviors.

Take singing lessons, even if you're tone deaf. Singing is good for the soul.

Use your best china every day—don't wait for the perfect moments that never arrive. Serve a peanut butter sandwich on Grandma's finest.

Gag your internal critic and never let it put you down.

Accept that creative blocks happen sometimes and recognize the positive in them: they make you appreciate your creativity even more when it returns.

Change the pictures in all the photo frames in your house.

Join clubs. It's good to be someone who participates.

Write a poem to your true love, whether you're with the person or not.

Put together a few eccentric outfits for days when you want to stand out from the crowd.

Design and create a garden—or roof terrace or window box—of your own.

Create sense memories of beautiful places you can call up at will.

Live your life in a fully awake state (except when you're in bed at night).

"Realize that now, in this moment of time, you are creating. You are creating your next moment. That is what's real. "

SARA PADDISON

upgrade your
attitude

Take comfort in the fact that forty is the best of all ages. You've still got your looks, but now you've got the wisdom to know what to do with them.

Understand that most problems are resolved without the need for action.

Forgive your parents for any grievances you have about your childhood.

Get over sibling rivalry, or friendship rivalry, or any other kind of unhealthy competitiveness.

Learn to look beyond words and actions to the motives that lie behind them.

Figure out who you can and can't trust in the world and how to tell the difference.

Choose a handful of people whose advice you trust; be sure to ask for advice when you need it.

Remember, in every situation you have choices. Even a prisoner shackled in a tiny cell can choose what he thinks about and the way he manages to keep going.

> "The pessimist sees difficulty in every opportunity. The optimist sees the opportunity in every difficulty."
>
> WINSTON CHURCHILL

Learn to spot the bad guys, and give them a wide berth.

Pay attention to coincidences; they often happen for a reason.

Live on your own for a while, so you know how to do it—even if you choose not to.

Be on the right track, but remember that you'll get run over if you just sit there.

66 **As I grow older, I pay less attention to what men say. I just watch what they do.** 99
ANDREW CARNEGIE

Make sure you're spending your life the way you want; you only get one life to live and you're almost halfway through it now.

66 *They say that time changes things, but you actually have to change them yourself.* 99
ANDY WARHOL

Learn how to step outside your own skin and understand how you appear to others

Volunteer to take part in a local play or musical—it's a great way to practice not taking yourself too seriously!

" The one important thing I have learned over the years is the difference between taking one's work seriously and taking one's self seriously. The first is imperative and the second disastrous. "
MARGOT FONTEYN

Learn to distinguish between productive and non-productive worry; ditch the latter.

Find ways of cheering yourself up when you're down.

Take the plunge and try some form of personal therapy; this will allow you to deal with your issues and move forward unencumbered.

Don't forget to smell the roses.
No one on his deathbed ever
said he wished he had spent
more time at work.

I have learnt silence from the talkative,
toleration from the intolerant, and
kindness from the unkind; yet strange,
I am ungrateful to these teachers.
KAHLIL GIBRAN

Make a list of your past mistakes and errors of judgment. Have a ceremonial burning of the paper, symbolically and finally forgiving yourself.

Learn how to see through con
artists and "special offers"
that cost an arm and a leg.

Know how to hire builders, plumbers,
and electricians and how to deal with
them so they achieve the results you want.

Give up any self-destructive habits
of your youth; replace them with a
few new quirky ones.

Read The Hitchhiker's Guide to the
Galaxy, *by Douglas Adams. If you've*
read it before, then read it again.

Write the story of your life in two pages,
with the second page being your future.

Stop letting anyone make you feel inferior;
they can only do it if you give them permission.

*Learn to look ahead for the open
door rather than staring backward
at the closed one. When one door
closes, another always opens.*

Understand that the finest moments come out
of periods when we are deeply unhappy or
unfulfilled; it is only then that we step out of
our ruts and start looking for different ways.

*Find your personal power
and start exerting it.*

" Learn how to be happy with what you
have while you pursue all that you want. "
JIM ROHN

Make sure you spend more time being happy than miserable. By our late thirties we tend to spend more time being one or the other— and misery isn't much fun.

Ask yourself a question: Do you respect yourself? If not, why? Is there anything you can do to change this?

Allow yourself to lose your dignity. It's an overrated virtue anyway.

Master ways of resolving conflict. Don't cut what could be untied.

Find a way to save an hour every day, and then decide how to spend it.

Try beating a pillow with your fists when something makes you angry.

"Learn to get in touch with silence within yourself, and know that everything in this life has a purpose. There are no mistakes, no coincidences. All events are blessings given to us to learn from. "
ELISABETH KUBLER-ROSS

Be sure you have a healthy way of dealing with stressful situations, whether it's exercise, deep breathing, meditation, or hugging a pet.

Always dance as if no one were watching you and remember that no matter what you've been through, you should try to love as if you have never been hurt.

Have you ever thought you would like to go back and relive your twenties and thirties knowing what you know now? You can!

Cultivate a reputation for throwing good parties. That way, everyone will want to come to the next one.

Smile because something happened; don't cry because it's over.

Become a mentor to someone
you can help, such as someone
who recently graduated from
college and who wants to have
a career in your industry.

Revise the criteria you use to make decisions.

When the going gets tough,
see if you can stop for a rest.

*" To hold the same views at forty as
we held at twenty is to have been
stupefied for a score of years, and
take rank, not as a prophet, but as
an unteachable brat, well birched
and none the wiser. "*
ROBERT LOUIS STEVENSON

Make sure you spend enough time with older members of your family while you still can. Find out what makes them tick.

Learn to challenge orthodox thinking, which encourages inhibitions and blind conformity. Look behind the messages of politicians, journalists, and even the Church, to find what you consider to be the truth.

Question the source of news you read in your morning paper. Where did it come from and how reliable is it?

" Experience is simply the name we give to our mistakes. "
OSCAR WILDE

Make a list of all your memories before the age of five. The more you think about it, the more memories you'll come up with.

Read a book or take a class on creative visualization. Discover the astonishing power of positive images.

Write to your favorite teacher in school and tell them what you appreciated.

Watch your favorite actor performing live on stage.

Go to a comedy club and be prepared for an evening of belly laughs.

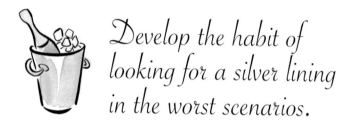 *Develop the habit of looking for a silver lining in the worst scenarios.*

"Our greatest glory is not in never falling, but in rising every time we fall."
CONFUCIUS

Be aware of the words and phrases you overuse, and try to change them from time to time.

Make sure you recognize and
celebrate milestones along the way.

"How you spend your time is more
important than how you spend your
money. Money mistakes can be
corrected, but time is gone forever."
DAVID NORRIS

Be your own life coach.
Take stock of your work life,
home life, love life, friendships,
and overall happiness and decide
what changes need to be made.

Let go of negative emotions. Hatred
damages the hater, anger harms the angry,
and grudges poison those who hold them.

*Read the newspaper from cover to cover,
including the pages you'd normally skip.*

*Familiarize yourself with the political
situation in another country.*

" People grow through experience if
they meet life honestly and courageously.
This is how character is built. "
ELEANOR ROOSEVELT

*Realize that you don't need to impress
anyone except yourself anymore.*

Understand that ultimately we all have
responsibility for our own happiness.

Choose a subject you feel strongly about, then create an argument for the opposite point of view.

> For a long time it had seemed to me that life was about to begin...But there was always some obstacle in the way. Something to be got through first, some unfinished business, time still to be served, a debt to be paid....At last it dawned on me that these obstacles were my life.

ALFRED D'SOUZA

Stop taking on other people's problems as your own to the extent that they hold you back.

Take a class or read a book about ways to improve your memory.

Learn to fix a dripping tap.

Know how to fix a blown fuse in your fuse box.

Buy a dictionary and a thesaurus, and use them to keep expanding your vocabulary.

Learn to stand up for yourself. If need be, take an assertiveness training course.

Develop the ability to get what you want from people in positions of authority. Polite firmness is often the best bet.

Learn to express your anger; suppressing it will make you old before your time.

"Until you make peace with who you are, you'll never be content with what you have."

DORIS MORTMAN

Feel free to cry when you need to— it's a healthy emotional release.

Figure out what makes you angry and why.

Accept that you are not superhuman. Perfectionism leads to burnout.

Recognize that completing a crossword puzzle
and getting a sauce to thicken are just as much
achievements as closing a big multinational deal.

Stop being afraid.
You've gotten this far, and it
hasn't all been plain sailing,
so believe you'll be able to
deal with whatever life throws
at you in the future.

Spend your time the way you want
to—it is the hard currency of life.
Don't let other people spend it for you.

Make sure you know how to change
a tire or check the oil in your car.

Resolve to play more. All work and no play makes you a dull person.

Know who you are, but don't get stuck with a rigid definition.

Walk a mile in someone else's shoes.

Learn to avoid saying "I can't." Better to say "I won't" or, better still, "I'll try."

Break through any crystallized patterns and mind-sets, otherwise they'll age you before your time.

Know that true intelligence is completely different from IQ.

Remember this: the most intelligent people in the world are the ones who are aware of how little they know.

Learn to keep things in perspective and don't expend too much energy worrying about the small stuff.

Understand that whether you are happy or miserable doesn't depend on the circumstances, but on how you approach them.

"For the first half of your life, people tell you what you should do; for the second half, they tell you what you should have done."
RICHARD NEEDHAM

Find a way to work flexible hours.

refresh your soul

Learn to enjoy each moment to the fullest.

Make the most of every opportunity.

Stop being envious of anyone else on the planet and be happy to be you.

Rejoice that thorns have roses rather than complain that roses have thorns.

Visit an ancient temple or holy site from a religion that is not yours, and sit peacefully, experiencing the calm.

Light a candle in a place of worship that is not your own and pray for someone you love (even if you are not religious).

Read first-person accounts of life in a World War II concentration camp, and think about the men who walked through the barracks comforting others, giving away their last pieces of bread.

Get your astrological chart made, your fortune told, or your tarot cards read.

Repay any karmic debts now that you are forty. If someone once did a huge favor for you, do the same for someone else.

> " There are only two ways to live your life. One is as though nothing is a miracle. The other is as though everything is a miracle. "
> ALBERT EINSTEIN

Retain childlike qualities, even if you have children.

Go on a silent retreat, during which you have no contact with the outside world, for a week.

Visit someone in the hospital and take them a thoughtful gift. Think about what you would want to receive.

Learn the art of meditation to help you stay calm in times of stress.

Sleep under the stars somewhere remote, away from the sounds of civilization.

Make sure you can live without your cell phone.

Be sure you have tried each of the
seven deadly sins: greed, sloth, lust,
pride, gluttony, anger, and envy.

Make your own list of seven sins and seven virtues.

*Spend a day in a nursing
home and encourage residents
to share their life stories.*

*Go to a spirit medium and see if the person
can contact any of your dead relatives.*

Consider whether you believe in karma. If it is true that your actions now can affect your future, are you happy with the way you are living?

Try asking a question of the Chinese oracle I Ching.

Forgive those who have hurt you in the past and move forward without bitterness.

Jettison any personal mythologies that are holding you back; exchange predetermination for free will.

> We grow old by deserting our ideals. Years may wrinkle the skin, but to give up enthusiasm wrinkles the soul.
> SAMUEL ULLMAN

Visit a sacred site at the summer solstice and light some candles.

Visit a prehistoric site and try to imagine what early man was thinking when he built it.

Look at a chart of the different periods of geological time and consider how recently mankind appeared on the scene.

Don't obsess about the afterlife;
accept that there are things we will
never understand in this world.

Throw coins in a fountain.

Choose a couple of worthy
charities and agree to a monthly
donation—whatever you can afford.

Visit a shelter for the homeless and
listen to the extraordinary life stories
of those who are staying there.

Know that it really is possible to change the world if you care enough.

Understand that the essence of intelligence is the ability to extract meaning from everyday experience.

"Nothing worth knowing can be understood with the mind."
WOODY ALLEN

Sponsor a child in a foreign country, and write to them regularly.

Until you value yourself,
you will not value your
time. Until you value your
time, you will not do
anything with it.
M. SCOTT PECK

Remember, only quiet waters give an
undistorted reflection and only quiet minds
see the world as it really is.

Still your ego and learn to approach
new situations with humility.

Never close your mind to
learning something new.

Sign up for a vacation in which you do volunteer work somewhere else in the country or world, and use your skills to change the lives of others.

Perform an anonymous act of kindness. Leave a bouquet of flowers at someone's front door, or slip a gift certificate into someone's shopping bag.

Look back at your past and identify your biggest regret. Can you make up for it now?

Make a list of what you take for granted, and then question everything.

Learn how to rise above pettiness.

Describe your personality in a paragraph or two. Does the description make you happy?

Give up something you enjoy for Lent, even if you are not religious.

Attend the birth of a baby. Savor the introduction of a new life.

Look at your own baby pictures and contemplate
the journey you have taken since then.

*Be a generous host or
hostess, and make your
hospitality renowned.*

Help strangers in need.
It might be you one day.

*Make the most of your regrets...
To regret deeply is to live afresh.*
HENRY DAVID THOREAU

Learn to shift gears. Set aside some time at the end of the day to be alone with your thoughts.

Embrace your spirituality, but before you recommit to your childhood religion or embrace another faith, examine it fully.

Understand that sometimes the belief comes first. You'll never see fairies if you don't believe in them.

Consider whether your rank, position, wealth, or status is important to you. Then recognize its irrelevance in the greater scheme of things.

Recall an insecure period of your childhood. Remember the things that troubled you. Now reach back over the decades, with the wisdom you have now, and tell that little child everything is going to be okay.

Think about what you consider to be your greatest weakness. Could it really be one of your greatest strengths?

It's not true that nice guys finish last. Nice guys are winners before the game even starts.
ADDISON WALKER

Keep your eyes open to all the valuable
life lessons that will help you evolve to
a higher spiritual plane.

Declare an amnesty at age forty, forgiving everyone who has wronged you in the past.

Learn to stop and listen to your
inner dialogue from time to
time; if it is negative, counter
it with positive affirmations.

Reclaim your childhood capacity for living entirely
in the present moment. It's never too late!

Make friendships a priority—and be a good friend. Note in your diary important upcoming events in your friends' lives and always call to wish them luck or see how things went.

Analyze the way your time is allocated among work, leisure, loved ones, and friends. Do you have the balance about right, or can you shift it?

Make your home the kind of place where people feel comfortable and welcome.

Learn to laugh at yourself and accept teasing.

Remember that no matter how crazy your family makes you, it's the only one you've got.

" No act of kindness, no matter how small, is ever wasted. "

AESOP

Instead of thinking about how to reach the next rung of the career ladder, consider whether you are on the right ladder.

Let go of your ego, and learn to accept rejection and criticism as a path to learning.

Make honesty a goal, and resolve
to start telling the truth now.

*Do a favor for someone
else——and do something nice
for yourself——every day.*

**Keep looking for the humor in
everyday life. The more you
look, the more you'll find.**

*Change your daily habits;
go to work a different way.*

Try to stop judging others. None of us are perfect.

Get lost. Take a road you've never taken before and wander down it without a plan.

Live by your instincts and let them be your divining rod. They represent an awareness of the world that goes beyond the five senses.

Nurture yourself by spending time with friends who are kind, thoughtful, compassionate, and considerate.

Think positive. Negative thoughts set up roadblocks on your route to achieving your goals.

Ask for miracles and believe they can happen.

Mahatma Gandhi said, "My life is my message." Does your life have a message?

Make a list of your good points——your skills, personality, achievements, even your appearance. Reread it whenever you need a boost.

Learn to stop wasting time on problems that can't be solved. Shift your focus.

Be able to admit you are wrong, and see things from another person's point of view. It's the only way you will ever sustain a loving relationship.

Stand up to a bully; speak out against a fraud; fight off a rival for a prize; care enough about something to make someone mad.

Is there someone in your life who frequently drives you crazy? Work out the negative dynamic. What buttons are they pressing?

Have a conversation with a celebrity. What did you learn? Are famous people any different?

Think of the best present you've ever been given. Have you said thank you?

Read up on auras, and try to see the color fields that surround us all.

Learn to use the healing powers of your hands: rub a child's sore stomach or massage a headache away.

The aim of life is self-development.
To realize one's nature perfectly—
that is what each of us is here for.
OSCAR WILDE

Make sure there are at least ten people you love and that they all know it.

Arrange a get-together with friends and bring out a Ouiji board. Open your mind to what might happen.

Peel your own onion and find the inner "you" underneath the layers of experience that have built up over the years.

Think about your higher self.
Do you have any idea what that is?

Vow to walk barefoot on grass, touch the earth with your bare skin, or smell a flower every day.

Walk in sunlight every day, especially in winter.

Think about someone you know who's unhappy and consider whether there's anything you can do to help—even if it's just a concerned phone call— every morning when you wake up.

Learn to double-check your motives before confronting a friend or family member about something that's been annoying you.

Try to focus and pick up spiritual messages. They're much more subtle than those from the material world.

"*You don't stop laughing because you grow old. You grow old because you stop laughing.*"
MICHAEL PRITCHARD

Consider what you can do that will leave the world a better place. Rescue a lost soul, write a beautiful piece of music, or do a good job of raising a child?

Cultivate a friendship with someone who is older than yourself—it helps you stay feeling young!

 Have a major purge of possessions and give at least a tenth of your things to charity.

Nurture your imagination and never fail to appreciate it.

Never lose touch with Nature.
Even in the heart of a big city, be aware of the sky and watch the birds.

Accept that uncertainty is one of the few certainties.

Have a friend who is much wiser than you, so you remember how much in life you don't yet know.

Remember that the universe is always in a state of balance; a problem cannot exist without its solution existing at the same time.

Find out what the true purpose of your life should be. Guided meditation or hypnosis might help you.

*Your life lies before you
like a path of driven snow,
be careful how you tread it
'cause every step will show.*
LOWRI WILLIAMS

Count all your blessings
on your birthday.

*Try to fit a life-enhancing experience into each day,
even if it's just a good conversation on the telephone.*

Discard any extra
baggage you are carrying.

Contemplate what you are serious
about and how you can lighten up.
According to Native American folklore,
the first question we ask after dying is,
"Why was I so serious?"

*Find things that make you laugh
and surround yourself with them.*

*Write down your personal
mission statement, follow it,
and revise it from time to time.*

" Blessed are those who can laugh
at themselves, for they shall
never cease to be amused. "
ANONYMOUS

Choose the five key values you believe in most strongly. Being aware of them will make decisions easier.

Keep your eyes open for new opportunities; don't let any slip by unnoticed.

Change the energy flow in your house with one simple exercise. Enter each room and clap your way around the periphery then out through the door. Try to follow the flow of air as you continue doing this through the house. Notice the change.

Consider downshifting and living a simpler life with fewer material possessions than you are used to.

Start to recycle your garbage. Improving the environment starts at home.

Smile at everyone you pass in the street for one day.

Keep asking those unanswerable questions.

Cancel an evening out and donate the money you would have spent to charity.

Cry at a sad movie, especially if you're not the crying type.

Put right a wrong you did long ago.

Give yourself permission to change your mind about everything.

Write down your five biggest strengths and your five worst weaknesses.

*Invite someone to spend
a holiday with you who
would otherwise be alone.*

" *Don't take life too
seriously. You'll
never get out alive.* "
BUGS BUNNY

Pick up someone else's litter.

Resolve not to opt for comfort and
security above the thrill of the unknown;
that is a middle-aged state of mind.

Eat humble pie.

Confront your fears.
Know everything's
going to be okay.

"Find an aim in life before you run out of ammunition."

ARNOLD GLASGOW

re-evaluate your relationships

Give someone a present they will cherish forever.

Collect half a dozen excellent jokes you can tell when the opportunity arises.

Have a relationship your mother would disapprove of.

Serenade someone from outside their bedroom window.

Learn not to shrink from
extravagant displays of affection.

*Have your heart broken at
least once—but not too often.*

" As long as you can still be
disappointed, you are still young. "
SARAH CHURCHILL

*Keep a secret none of your
closest friends and family
know, and that would surprise
them if they found out.*

Learn someone else's likes and dislikes and pander to their tastes.

Show someone you love them rather than just telling them.

Make a friend from each of the five continents.

Have at least one friend in each decade: under ten, teenage, twenties, thirties, and so on up to a hundred.

Throw a party for
more than fifty people.

Go to wedding ceremonies of people from different
cultures and see how they celebrate their love.

Open your heart to
someone completely and
utterly, without reservation.

Make changes now if you keep repeating the
same negative patterns in relationships; think
about getting some counseling to help you.

" What you leave behind is not what is engraved in stone monuments, but what is woven into the lives of others. "
PERICLES

Throw away your teenage fantasies of perfect love and eternal romance, and realize that an honest, feet-on-the-ground, reciprocal relationship is much more fulfilling.

Surprise someone by sending them a mystery Valentine's card.

Think about what your friends like most about you. Be sure not to disappoint them.

Reconnect with any old friends you miss.

Organize a school reunion. Remember to make name badges in case people don't recognize one another.

Make friends with people from outside your normal sphere—with jobs and backgrounds very different from yours.

Find out more about your genes. If you're adopted, trace your birth mother; if not, do some research into your family tree.

Face up to your responsibilities; at forty, you are the pivot between the oldest and youngest members of your family.

Resolve disputes with older family members; you never know how much longer they will be around.

Plan something unusual for your next birthday party. Can you have it in a haunted castle or on a yacht?

Try to make a match between a pair of carefully chosen single friends.

Stop yourself from putting up barriers, no matter how much you've been hurt. Leave yourself wide open.

Be a mediator between two people who have had a falling out.

Learn to listen to both sides of an argument.

Live with a partner and learn about all the compromises, considerations, nuances, and joys of cohabitation.

Separate from your family enough to become yourself.

Identify your unique charms and use them shamelessly.

Stop worrying about what others think of you. Just make sure you think highly of yourself.

Learn to make up before the end of the day.

Don't be too proud to make the first move.

Steer clear of people who scoff at your dreams.

Weed out any false friends—
the charlatans and users.

Have a really good put-down ready for anyone who is outrageously rude to you.

> **The first problem for all of us, men and women, is not to learn, but to unlearn.**
> GLORIA STEINEM

Make up a little black book (or big one, if necessary) with photos of everyone you've ever dated.

Fantasize about the most romantic vacation you can possibly imagine. Then consider how you can make it come true.

> *Change everything except your loves.*
> *VOLTAIRE*

Ask friends at a dinner party
what they think people should
do now that they're forty.
It's a great conversation starter!

Be a good raconteur. Learn how to make a story
amusing, and include just the right amount of detail.

Have a friend who
will tell you when
you're being
unreasonable or
downright foolish.

Have at least one friend who is
always the life of the party.

Find out the history of your surname. Does it mean you belong to a clan or a tribe?

Why not try a life swap? Spend a day in someone else's shoes and let them spend a day in yours.

Do something your friends would consider totally out of character.

Look up your first-ever girlfriend or boyfriend and flirt outrageously with him or her.

> *The lovely thing about being forty is that you can appreciate twenty-five-year-old men.*
> COLLEEN McCULLOUGH

Get in the habit of talking to cab drivers and people you regularly sit next to on the way to work.

Visit a Web site that helps you search for friends from high school or college.

Be aware of the methods you use to get new people to like you. Use them.

Put down roots in a community so even if you don't stay there forever, you'll always belong.

Get involved with children's activities, such as coaching a sports team or volunteering at a school whether or not you have children.

Make sure that no matter how many things you are called in your life, "boring" is never one of them.

Resolve to make at least one new friend a year. If you haven't made a new one when you're forty, do it quickly and invite the person to your forty-first birthday party.

Stay in touch with pop culture. Ask a teenager to explain the latest jargon, and to tell you the coolest bands and clothing styles.

Develop a habit of complimenting friends on something every time you see them.

Invent a new word and keep using it until you get someone else to adopt it.

Start a harmless but fun rumor; whisper it to a friend and see how long it takes to get back to you via a different route.

Confront a bully and make the person feel small.

Scream at someone at the top of your lungs.

Run the length of a railway platform and fling yourself into someone's arms, just like in the movies.

Become more tactile. Kiss and hug friends and family when you greet them and when you say good-bye.

Give someone a hug for no reason and feel their pleasure.

> When I passed forty I dropped pretense,
> 'cause men like women who got some sense.
MAYA ANGELOU

Tell your parents you love them, especially if you haven't said it recently.

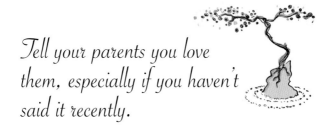

Make sure you know your relatives as people—not just as a father, aunt, or cousin.

Pay a surprise visit to a relative who lives far away.

Spend time watching a newborn——your own or someone else's——and imagining the world as they experience it.

Visit with someone who is wheelchair-bound and try to understand the problems they face.

Surround yourself with people who laugh at your jokes.

Go on a blind date. Everyone should try this at least once. Even better, kiss your date on first meeting the person.

Share your most precious dreams with someone special, and see if they would like to join you.

Play a game of strip poker with someone to whom you are very attracted.

Ask someone you've only just met for a date.

Feed someone ice cream as they lie back in a hot bath.

Start a savings account for a favorite child and present it to them on an important birthday.

Update your telephone and address book.

Watch the James Stewart movie It's a Wonderful Life *and look back on all the ways in which you have affected those around you.*

Teach a child how to whistle.

Meet your parents on an adult level. As you get older, you will start to notice that you have a lot in common with them; use these insights to open the door to a new, mature relationship.

Know your neighbors.

" We cannot live only for ourselves. A thousand fibers connect us with our fellow men; and among those fibers, as sympathetic threads, our actions run as causes, and they come back to us as effects. "

HERMAN MELVILLE

Start a notebook of unique family sayings and traditions.

Keep a record of cute and funny things said by the children in your life.

Tell someone they are the most beautiful person in the world.

Try to change the opinion of someone who dislikes you.

Fall in love during your fortieth year.
If you are already in love, find a way
to take these feelings to a deeper level.

Make an imaginative will with
lots of individual bequests that
will make the recipients smile.

Are you married? If not,
do you know who you
would like to marry?
Bite the bullet and propose!

Come clean and confess to a lie
you've told, no matter how innocent.

Find the person who is your touchstone.

Try speed dating if you're not in a relationship but would like to be.

Make sure you are close to someone else's children if you don't have kids of your own.

Collect photographs of your favorite people.

Always err on the
side of generosity.

Make sure there's someone in your
life you can call at 3:00 A.M.

Be brave enough to tell a
friend when you think they're
making a huge mistake.

Think about the advice you would give to an
eighteen-year-old who was leaving home for the
first time. Have you taken it yourself?

Make time for your friends whenever they need it.

Give someone an appropriate nickname.

Never give up having crushes.

Have at least one great love affair before you turn fifty. Give yourself to it completely, even if it turns out they are not the person you are destined to spend the rest of your life with.

Learn how to leave relationships before they get bitter and nasty.

Ask siblings, if you have them, how they remember your childhood. Their memories are probably different from yours.

Ask your parents what they would do differently if they had their lives to live over again.

Keep a book of birthdays so you never forget an important one.

Make a loved one a tape or CD of music that means something to both of you.

Help a friend move or decorate their home.

Sit up all night talking with someone.

Take a ride in a tunnel of love and kiss in the dark.

Keep a memory trunk for all those precious cards and letters.

Send a surprise bouquet to a close relative, for no reason at all.

Make sure you've danced with a lover until dawn at least once.

Back up all the numbers stored in your cell phone.

> *There is more hunger for love and appreciation in this world than for bread.*
> MOTHER TERESA

Record your elderly relatives' earliest memories on tape.

Go through elderly relatives' photo albums and make sure they've told you who everyone is.

Make your parents proud of you.

Tell each of your
friends what you
admire about them.

Give praise where praise is due.

Say anything left unsaid that still
rankles. Do it now, in a letter.

*Choose friends who bring sanity
rather than chaos into your life.*

Find a secret fantasy person for daydreams in quiet moments.

Make friends with someone who is your opposite in every way.

Prove yourself to be a good secret keeper.

Ask someone out
purely on impulse.

Give as good as you get—or better.

Find out what happened to your best friend from primary school.

Get to know your friends' friends; it will reveal a lot about the people you know best.

Give homemade Christmas cards one year.

Cultivate any kindred spirits
you meet along the way.

Try to remember every detail of
the most romantic day of your life.

Write a letter to an old love you
haven't seen for at least five years.

If you have any long lost relatives
you would like to see again, try
entering the person's name in an
Internet search engine.

Get rid of anyone in your life who makes you feel worthless and depressed.

Ask each of your friends to teach you one new thing.

Make friends with everyone in your family.

Get ready to become a "parent" to your parents as they age.

Learn how to listen well and to hear what is not being said.

Realize that there is no such thing as a "normal" person. We are all peculiarly individual and distinct.

Plan a surprise for someone who deserves a treat.

Stop expecting anyone else in the world to look after you.

Comfort someone who has recently been bereaved.

Organize a family reunion and make it an event to remember.

Be a soul mate to someone and let them be yours.

Know that love matters more than anything else; in fact, nothing else really matters at all.

First Published in Great Britain in 2005 by Spruce,
a division of Octopus Publishing Company Ltd
Endeavour House, 189 Shaftesbury Avenue, London WC2H 8JY
www.octopusbooksusa.com

An Hachette UK Company
www.hachette.co.uk

Distributed in the US by
Hachette Book Group USA, 237 Park Avenue,
New York NY 10017 USA

Distributed in Canada by
Canadian Manda Group, 165 Dufferin Street,
Toronto, Ontario, Canada M6K 3H6

ISBN: 978-1-84072-797-5

10 9

Printed and bound in China